# Textbook

# Annihilation

Webinar Transcript

Textbook Annihilation: Everything There Is To Know About Profiting From Textbooks

First paperback edition published 2019 by Mastery Media.

All rights reserved. No part of this book or site may be reproduced or redistributed in any form or by any electronic or mechanical means, including information storage and retrieval systems, without permission in writing from the author and publisher, except by a reviewer who may quote brief passages in a review.

Copyright © 2019 Peter Valley

www.FBAmastery.com

peter@fbamastery.com

Welcome to Textbook Annihilation – everything there is to know about profiting from textbooks.

I'm going to attempt to teach you every single thing I know about textbooks in one class. So I am going to go rapid fire through what I think is everything you need to know and if there's somehow by any chance there's any stone I leave unturned, we're going to go through Q&A and it's going to be a blast.

## What You're Going To Learn

Okay, so here are **the three pillars of textbook season profits** and textbook season in general.

**Number one is what I'm calling textbook intelligence.** This is essentially every little bit of detail that you need to know about textbooks to understand what drives the textbook market. This is getting a deep knowledge of how textbooks work and all the different factors at play on how they sell, what buyers want. It's kind of a catch-all category encompassing what you need to know about the textbook market to get sales.

**Number two is textbook pricing.** This is massive. This is where you stand to make and lose the most amount of money with textbooks. This subject isn't exciting, but it is really key.

**Number three is textbook sourcing.** I.e. where to find the textbooks. So if you have these three things locked in, you are basically guaranteed to make a killing not just during textbook season but on Amazon in general.

So with that understanding, what do you say we move forward?

## About Me

So let's get to know each other just a little bit.

In this picture you see here on the right is my response to make amends for times in the past when I did these webinars, and used deceiving photos that gave me the appearance of legitimacy. Which I admit now is a complete ruse. So I decided in the interest of honesty and transparency to actually let you know what I really look like and act like on a moment-by-moment basis. And that's a photo of me looking like a complete doofus which is a more accurate representation of who I am.

So my name is Peter Valley. I've been selling on Amazon since 2007. I've been called both a

"Leading expert on internet bookselling" and, "Hey everybody, don't follow his blog. There's more important things than money." Somebody sent me a screenshot of this on Facebook, and I think it's awesome when your critics actually tacitly admit that you, yes, your advice will make people money but you still shouldn't follow them. It's like, "Yeah, his stuff works but you still shouldn't follow him anyway." That's how you know you're doing good.

So I'm the creator of fbamastery.com. An online sourcing automation tool called Zen Arbitrage. A bunch of free webinars that people keep telling me I should charge for but I'm apparently not the most savvy business person.

I'm the author of many books on Amazon seller such as *Amazon Autopilot, Book Sourcing Secrets* and literally ten other books and course that I haven't released for no real reason other than that I lack the discipline and motivation to get them out into the public.

Okay, so with all of that self-deprecation out of the way, let's forget what I've done. Let's talk what motivates me.

When I'm on these webinars and I listen to these people teach stuff I'm always like, "Why are you here, man? What drives you?" So I just want to let you know kind of where I'm coming from.

**Why Sell On Amazon?**

Why am I here? I am 100% percent firmly unapologetically against working for anyone else. That's why I sell on Amazon. That's why I do what I do and my goal is to help you achieve that level of freedom as well.

I think the highest and most noble of all personal goals is freedom. So that's what selling with FBA stuff this webinar is all about. I just kind of want to give you the philosophical underpinnings of all of this stuff because that's something I think most teachers don't talk about.

**My Promise For This Webinar**

I want to make one promise to you before we get started. I really do believe that your time is your most precious asset. It's way, way, way more valuable than money. If I came into your house, and I won't unless you leave the key and give me your address, but if I came to your house and took all your money, okay, you could replace that. But you can never, ever, ever get your time back including the hour that you're going to spend with me.

So it is my promise that anytime I ask for a little bit of your time that I will do everything

I can to deliver the most amount of value possible. Because I believe very strongly that you should maybe forgive somebody who is reckless with your money but you should never ever forgive anyone who is reckless with your time.

If you guys are cool with me doing the very best that I can to make this worth your time, what do you say we get started.

## Webinar Synopsis

Here's what you will learn by the end of this webinar.

You're going to get a deep knowledge of textbooks, how to price textbooks for maximum profits, the best sources of textbooks, and we're going to do tons of Q&A. I'm willing to go as long as we have to. I would prefer to get to sleep and have some dinner at some point but I'll go as long as we have to.

## My Humble Beginnings

So now you know these guys that get on the internet and they're like, "I've been selling on Amazon for a hundred years and I make $100 million and you should listen to me." Okay, so I hate that stuff.

I started out as literally the worst seller. I say started out, I may in fact still hold this title, as the worst, most inefficient Amazon seller ever. So whatever you've done wrong, I've done it worse, believe me.

I remember back in the day when I first got started, I lived in LA. I used to drive 45 minutes to garage sales because I saw an ad of Craigslist that said, "Hey, we got a box of computer books for $10." I have these horrific memories of driving through the hundred degree heat in the San Gabriel Valley hunting down books that were almost always a complete flop. I drove an hour to buy three boxes of computer books from the 1990s, and this is deep in the 2000s.

I skateboarded almost everyday, 30 minutes to a college dumpster, every single day, that only had books maybe 1 out of 5 times I went. And in the event that I found books in their dumpster, I had to literally skateboard home with the box, carrying the box or wheeling it on my skateboard. I mean these are some tough times, you guys. This is what I used to do.

I spent my first year as an Amazon seller, keying in books manually on my flip phone. I could go and on.

I wasted countless hours following advice from these fake gurus who as I found out later didn't even sell on Amazon. I lost thousands of dollars on bad inventory because I just didn't know my numbers.

I let a bunch of internet weirdos early on in my career...you know those people on Facebook who just spread a bunch of nonsense? I let them deter me from profitable tactics and I learned that for every good idea there is, there's going to be a hundred people on Facebook who are going to tell you you're wrong, I've had to find out the hard way.

So the point is, everything you can do wrong, I've done wrong.

At the end, you are going to feel very liberated if you don't practice this material already. You're going to feel very liberated when you learn these things because I'm your canary in a coal mine. I have went ahead and took the risks and made all the mistakes. And I'm here to tell you some things that a lot of people don't believe about textbooks, but once they experience them, they end up feeling very freed in terms of the emotional and time burden that these false beliefs bring to bear on them.

This webinar will be both profitable and liberating.

# Textbook Pillar I

# Textbook Intelligence

# Textbook Pillar #1: Textbook Intelligence

Number one is textbook intelligence. And this is the one you're probably wondering what the heck is Peter Valley talking about? Well, textbook intelligence, here's how I define it:

Textbook intelligence is:

*"The complete body of knowledge to identify textbooks, understand the textbook buyer and understand the market forces that drive sales."*

And if that sounds totally academic, let's just put you at ease. This will all make sense very shortly. So here's what we're going to cover...

- We're going to cover the myth of textbook season.
- What textbook buyers care about.
- What textbook buyers don't care about.
- Do older edition sell?
- Condition and textbooks.
- "Textbooks in disguise," and how to spot textbooks that aren't really textbooks.
- Where Amazon sellers lose the most money with textbooks.
- How to describe your textbooks.
- The peak days of textbook season.

..and a lot more.

**The Size Of The Textbook Market**

How big is the textbook market? Well, here are some hard numbers I pulled up for you. The total number of 2 and 4-year schools, meaning places with those weird buildings that I've never attended where people buy books, is 7,253. The total number of students, this actually surprised me, is 20 million people. That's under 10% of the total population, that's probably like 7%. But that is massive, massive, massive; because they buy way more books than the average person.

So the textbook market is massive. I mean those are some pretty staggering numbers. 20 million... I had no idea.

**Myths Of "Textbook Season"**

So lesson number one, textbook season is a myth. And it's partially my fault for spreading this, and for not speaking responsibly about what textbook season is. So let me explain. Let me try to undo some of the damage I may have done hyping up this thing called the "textbook season."

Okay, so here's how most Amazon sellers look at textbook season. They think, "Okay, this is the two times a year in August/September and then January when people buy textbooks." Okay, that's wrong. That's is not how the textbook market works.

Here's how we should look at textbook season and how, if I could go back, how I would be more careful in educating people about it:

*"The two times a year when the textbooks sales go up."*

Sales spike during textbook season. Textbooks don't *not* sell in the off-season. So it's more of a glass-half-full thing than glass-half-empty, and that's what people miss. Textbooks sell all year-round.

So if you are a little bit older than I am, you probably live in a world that doesn't exist anymore. There was a time when all school schedules and the higher education system in general was very uniform. Schools start at this time, they end at this time, everything was very uniform and you can kind of set your watch by when textbook sales would spike. And actually I'm going back even further than Amazon exists. But in theory, that's how you would have been able to do it some years ago.

But that world doesn't exist anymore. Between online courses and the general just increased variety in higher education, textbooks are selling all year round and it's happening more than ever. So it's really important to keep in mind that with textbook season, the highs aren't nearly as high as you might think they are and the lows and the off season are nearly as low.

So if you think textbooks are a seasonal business, again, you're living in a world that doesn't exist anymore. And that's actually a good thing because seasonal businesses are inherently unstable and I would never want to be in one. Granted, selling books on Amazon does not put us in purely the textbook business. I mean, the vast majority of the books I sell are not textbooks.

But I take comfort in knowing it is not seasonal. And a lot of people don't realize that so I wanted to kind of get that out of the way.

**The Biggest Sales Days For Textbook Season**

So here's the big question a lot of people ask: What are the peak days of textbook season? For fall semester, it's going to be the third full week of August.

For the fall semester, which is what we're coming up on, the third Monday in August is generally the biggest day of textbook sales day of them all.

Then followed by Tuesday and then followed by the Wednesday. That week, the third full week, is historically the biggest week for sales.

Sales mostly return to normal after the first week of September. So you're going roughly from August 15 to September 7th, if we had to be really general. And again, the days of the week factor in. So like if the 15th fell on a Saturday or Sunday, textbook sales are actually really slow on the weekends and then they go back up on the following Monday.

And then in spring semester, it's basically the first three days of January are the biggest sales days. And then sales mostly come to a stop after the third week of January. So were talking about mostly a 3-week window for textbook season for both fall semester and spring semester.

## The Most Misguided Textbook Questions

Here's what everybody wants to know, and these questions comes up a lot.

- How many textbooks will I sell during textbook season?
- What percentage of my textbooks will I sell during textbook season?
- How many textbooks do I need in my inventory to make X amount of dollars?

Do you know what I'm about to say? I bet you can guess.

*Every single one of these is asking the wrong question.*

It depends on too many factors. It depends on how you price, depends on the demand for your books, it depends how regularly you reprice, etc, etc.

So there's no way to answer these questions. Those questions are literally unanswerable. Even if I had a spreadsheet of all your books, I still couldn't answer that question for you. So you're simply asking the wrong questions.

What you should be asking is:

*"How can I focus on getting the highest quality inventory in the largest volume that I possibly can and then pricing it intelligently?"*

If you do those things the rest takes care of itself.

You have to focus on the things you can control, which is your inventory and your pricing, and let the rest take care of itself. Don't get caught up in, "Am I going to hit X amount of revenue?" Or, "I have to sell 70% of my textbooks or I'm going to freak out." None of those things matter. None of them can be controlled and none of them can be predicted. So you just focus on your inventory and pricing and the rest takes care of itself.

## Do Older Editions Of Textbooks Sell?

Another question that comes up: Do old textbooks sell? This is among the single most destructive question Amazon sellers get hung up on when it comes to textbooks. I certainly hear this all the time and it is a complete disaster of a question.

It's another one of those things where you are literally asking the wrong question. The age or edition of a textbook is not just a lesser data point, it is literally 100% completely totally irrelevant. And I can't overstate that enough.

The edition should not even be acknowledged because it will only serve to confuse you and it's meaningless. *One hundred percent meaningless.*

The only thing that matters when you're looking at a book decide if it's going to sell is the sales rank and more importantly, the sales rank history, that you can reveal through Keepa. That's all that matters.

Textbook edition is irrelevant. Don't acknowledge it, don't think about it, don't ask that question, don't even consider it. All that matters is sales rank.

So if you're holding a 12th edition of *Introduction To Biology*, published in 1998 or 1958 for that matter, and let's say that book is on its 326th edition. If the sales rank indicates it's selling then it's selling and that is it. All you do is defer to the data. That's it.

So I got into this email debate with somebody where it was like, they're asking me like, "Hey, what do you think of this book? Like, would you buy it?" I ran the ISBN in through Amazon and I was like, "Yeah." And they're like, "Well, I don't think it's going to sell." And I said, "Well, the sales rank's good. The sales rank history is good." And they said, "Look, it's an older edition and I just don't think people will buy it." And I said, "What does it matter what you think?" I was polite about it but I said, "It doesn't matter what you think. The sales rank history does not lie," and she just kind of figuratively crossed her arms and said, "No. I don't believe it and I don't believe you and I don't think it's going to sell because it's old." And I was like, "All right, have a blast with that." But people's unwillingness to sort of shut off their brains and just defer to the data costs them a lot of money.

So it doesn't matter what makes sense, it just matters what the data says.

On that subject, textbooks I've noticed become obsolete over years but not semesters. So one common myth is, "I'm worried that I'm going to buy these textbooks and then you know, maybe they're selling well now and the sales rank history is good now. But next semester, all the professors are going to stop assigning the book and I'm going to be stuck with worthless inventory."

That is not how it works. Textbook sales coast to a stop over years, not semesters. There's no textbook that is hot this semester that will be obsolete next semester. That is absolutely not how it works.

So college syllabuses are a very un-uniform thing. And remember, we're talking about 7,000 schools. There is no uniformity amongst how they create their syllabuses. And amongst those 7,000 universities, there is even untold more professors. So there is zero percent chance they're all getting together behind the scenes to conspire to make certain textbooks obsolete. So there's just no uniformity. Don't worry about that.

## What To Ignore When Pricing Textbooks

So when you're talking about textbook value, here's some factors that don't matter and hopefully this is somewhat reassuring to you.

One, rental price does not matter. I see people actually literally underpricing the rental price because they think if someone can rent a book for cheaper than they can buy it for, then they're not going to buy their copy. Say there's a book that's selling for $50 FBA and the rental price is $20, and they price it at $19.95, which is a huge mistake. It's dumb in the sense that it will cost you a lot of money.

So don't acknowledge rental price, don't acknowledge Kindle price. A lot of people try to underpriced Kindle. Total mistake. Don't look at other sites like eBay, don't worry about any of that.

Just assume, this is the rule of thumb, assume that your buyer is only looking at the page that your book is on. Does that make sense? So that means, to a certain extent you can even ignore, if you have a used copy, you can kind of even ignore the new copy. I won't say that is a hard and fast rule but I personally ignore everything that's not on that page. So hopefully, that makes sense.

## When Should You Ship Your Textbooks To Amazon?

Okay, so should you wait until August to ship your textbooks? And this is another question that comes up a lot that I wanted to address.

As I said earlier, seasonal businesses tend to not be sustainable. So my approach is I ship textbooks in whenever I get them and I price them what I call "unreasonably high." The better the rank, the more "unreasonable" I will price them.

I'm pricing in such a way that I don't really expect it to sell anytime soon, I don't care if it sells anytime soon. I'm basically pricing my textbooks for the textbook season environment, when prices and demand go up. So I price it for textbook season.

But here's the thing: A ton of my textbooks will sell before then. So I get the best of both worlds: I get sales in the off-season, but for textbook season prices. And I still get tons of sales for equally high prices during textbook season. Win-win.

So send your stuff in when you get it, price it unreasonably high, which is subjective, and a lot of your textbooks will sell before textbook season. Which is good because you're still getting a high price for them and then a lot more will sell during textbook season. So you get the best of all worlds. That is my approach.

## Ignore Sales Rank History From Mid-December

Here's another little tip that is very important, ignore all sales rank history from mid-December. Mid-December is starting around you know basically the 15th or so maybe 12th, give or take, and that is absolutely rock bottom in terms of textbook sales. Nobody is buying textbooks. They just got out of school and it's only time of the year when basically all schools agree nobody is in class. There's summer session at different times, there's spring break at different times. But nobody is in school on December 18th.

So textbook sales are absolutely rock bottom at that time. If you're looking at sales rank history data in Keepa, which you always should, you can safely discard any valleys of demand if they occur in mid to late December. So let's just say roughly the 15th to the 25th but that could even be the 10th through the 25th. A lot of sales do happen on the 26th because everybody in world gets gift cards on Christmas. So I would say, you know, roughly the 12th to the 25th, you can ignore any sales rank data during that period.

**What Matters To Textbook Buyers And What Doesn't**

Here's what does not matter very much with textbooks. And by the way, I don't what to be misinterpreted or misquoted as saying these things do not matter at all. I personally lean towards them not mattering at all but I don't want to get anyone in any kind of trouble so I'll just say they don't matter nearly as much as you probably they think they do.

**The Two Things That Don't Matter**

Inserts, most students do not care about inserts. The CD's, the access codes, and so on. It is not a concern for the vast majority textbook buyers and they understand when they buy a used book, they're probably not going to get inserts. As added insurance, Amazon actually warns buyers in the checkout process now to not expect inserts if they're buying a used book. So you have double insurance: The warning from Amazon, and students not caring that much anyway.

And then condition. Students have 1,000 things that occupy their minds. Tinder, getting drunk, fighting with roommates, or whatever. Whether the corner of the book they ordered is a little frayed and it wasn't mentioned in the Amazon listing is not in this list of top 1,000 things.

Those are the two biggest things that people overthink when it comes to textbooks: Inserts and condition.

Now what does matter, to some, is the absence of highlighting. I don't also want to be misquoted. It does not mean that books that have highlighting won't sell. I sell tons and tons of books that have tons and tons of highlighting. What it does mean is there is a certain percentage of textbook buyers that actively seek out books that don't have highlighting in them. And I'm going to tell you how to capitalize on that in just a second.

**Inserts And Access Cards**

So I pulled an actual statistic for you guys. I went deep into the numbers and I pulled up the average annual revenue that Amazon sellers lose because they're afraid to list textbooks that don't have all the inserts. Do you know what this figure is? You're probably wondering how the heck did he get this figure. I have an actual figure for you. This is the first of its kind. Are you ready? Let's drum roll it…

It is 100 bazillion trillion million kajillion billion bazillion.

That's a real number and I actually hacked into your phones and hacked into your cameras and watched you as you were sourcing and I figured out exactly how many books you're passing on because they don't have inserts and this is the actual figure.

Now I made this poor attempt at comedy just to drive home this point that this hang-up people have on inserts is completely destructive.

I never hesitate to list textbooks that don't have CDs or access codes. Nor do I mention their absence.

I will mention the *presence* of inserts. When they do exist, I do mention that because I think that could be a selling point even if the buyer doesn't intend to use them. I think people just kind of like to see that it's there and the seller took the time to actually grade the book and mention that stuff.

But I never hesitate to sell books without CDs or access codes nor do I ever mention their absence.

My experience is that almost nobody cares about access codes. I personally have never received bad feedback for sending a textbook out that didn't have an access code. It doesn't mean that some of you will not have another experience but personally, I've never gotten a bad feedback for that.

As bonus insurance, Amazon includes a disclaimer on textbook pages warning buyers that used books may not come with inserts. So you're protected on a couple of levels. One, that people understand used textbooks don't usually have the inserts and two, Amazon actually gives a disclaimer to filter out the people that do care saying, "Hey, there's a good chance you won't get that insert." So between those two things, you're pretty much covered.

You'll leave a lot of money on the table getting hung up on this.

## Condition

Here's another thing that doesn't matter as much for textbook buyers, is condition. And again, it doesn't mean it doesn't matter, it just means that it doesn't matter that much. It means it matters *less* than the average Amazon buyer.

You know how you get a lot of frivolous feedback if you're doing some volume on Amazon where people go, "I ordered a very good copy and I received a good copy." And you just kind of roll your eyes like, "Okay, great dude," and you have to work to get the feedback removed.

Generally the textbook buyer is not that picky. They're just looking for an intact book that is free of highlighting, and again, a lot of them don't even care about that.

But to the extent that they really care about condition, it's about highlighting. And they just want a book that's intact. These are college students, they're not sweating the details that much. So you can relax your grading standards just a little bit with textbooks. And I don't mean to be sloppy about it, just don't get too hung up on the details.

## What *Does* Matter To Textbook Buyers

So what does matter to textbook buyers? I think the biggest question textbook buyers ask is does it have highlighting or not? It doesn't mean all of them feel strongly about this but if they do feel strongly about it, they're probably combing through the listings and they're willing to pay more for a book that very clearly says "no highlighting." I'm not saying that most textbook buyers care that much, but the ones that do will pay more to avoid highlighting.

There is a really important way to capitalize on this. With all my textbooks, I put "no writing or highlighting" front and center in my condition description.

So what I'm doing is I am capitalizing on the people that do care about highlighting because most textbooks sellers don't actually mention if a book does not have highlighting. In fact, most textbooks always have that generic description that says "May include writing or highlighting" inside the book even when it doesn't have writing or highlighting. So you really give yourself an edge in getting those customers that do care about highlighting if you mentioned this front and center. That's a really profitable tip.

I just want to mention, highlighting is not a textbook death sentence. I actually have talked to some students and some actually *prefer* highlighting. Some of them, not most, but a few of them do because it means someone else has done the hard work for them. You know most students are going to have to do some highlighting on their own anyway so if someone else has already done it, they kind of appreciate that. So don't necessarily avoid a textbook just because it has highlighting.

## Spotting "Textbooks In Disguise"

Fact: Most textbooks don't actually look like textbooks. In fact, most books purchased by students don't look like textbooks at all.

There's two ways you can kind of define a textbook. One is, is it a format and is there a definition that we could apply to the format? Is it merely a specific size of book that is clearly for a college student? Is it merely the typical size and type of book that we think of as a "textbook"?

There's a definition I think which is more suitable for our purposes which is books that are purchased by students that we can command much higher prices for as FBA sellers. This defies subject matter. This defies format. This defies fiction of non-fiction.

That's the definition that I'm sticking to for the purpose of this slide, which is books that don't necessarily look like textbooks but are purchased by college students and have the demand among students such that we can get insanely higher prices for them.

So it can be really valuable to learn how to spot books that are subject to the same market forces but are in disguise. In other words, they don't look like a giant 7-inch by whatever the dimensions are, a 10-inch book that are 800 pages and hardcover and the whole thing that we think of when we think of a textbook. So these are books that don't look like textbooks, but we can still price really high and the demands all goes way up at the beginning of each semester. So it can really pay to learn how to spot these.

So here's a couple of tricks and there really is no sort of formula for this but here's a couple of tricks.

**Clue #1: Niche nonfiction that doesn't really have any real world application.** If you're kind of looking at this just being like, "Why the heck would somebody want a book about this," and it feels very academic, you know, like its on a university press or something along those lines. A rule of thumb is if it's on a subject that nobody won't care about if they weren't forced to care by a professor, that's probably a "textbook in disguise."

**Clue #2: Stickers indicating they were sold in a college bookstore.** Another way to spot a textbook in disguise is if you are out sourcing second-hand books, that have a giant square white sticker on the back. You know what I'm talking about, those textbooks sticker or any kind of markings that indicate it was sold through a university book store.

**Clue #3: Supplemental content for students.** Another little clue is a normal book that has supplemental material like annotations. Like this Jane Austen book on this slide here, you can see it says "annotated edition." That's a clue that this is going to be a book that's going to be purchased by students in a literature department, for example. The average Jane Austen reader is not going to want an annotated edition.

**Clue #4: nonfiction books that generally just appears scholarly and academic.** It can be a clue that they follow the same sort of market forces that drive textbook sales are going to apply to these books.

So it's really important because the majority, and I should have mentioned this at the beginning, but the majority of "textbooks" fit into this category that I just described. So it's really important to understand that textbooks most of the time don't look like textbooks. And I wish there was a formula I could give you. If you just look at all the clues you can generally get a pretty good idea.

If you really want to get deep, you know, I don't recommend spending this much time on any one book when you're sourcing but if you really want to get deep, you can actually you know look up a book's sales rank history and see how much it spikes during August or January and that will even give you a better clue.

Okay, so I just gave you what I think is a genius-level textbook IQ.

I taught you about textbook season, the peak days for textbook sales, the truth about older textbooks, what textbook buyers care about, what they don't, what matters most, and spotting textbooks in disguise.

# Textbook Pillar II

# Textbook Pricing

# Textbook Pillar #2: Textbook Pricing

So let's got to pillar number two. And this is where it's going to start to go a little bit faster because this stuff is not nearly as complex as what I just described.

First of all, textbook pricing is where you stand to make and or lose the most amount of money with textbooks. I would say this is possibly as important, there's really no way to kind of give it a hierarchy but let's say it's equally tied with sourcing with how important it is in terms of how much money you're going to make.

So why is textbook pricing important? Textbook pricing is second only to your inventory. It depends on what time of the year we are talking about, but second in what separates the people who make a lot of money from the people who just do okay. It's where most of your money is made and lost.

If you take two people who have 500 textbooks, one is going to make 3 times more than the other. So how's that possible? The answer is pricing.

I'm going to make the case with these examples.

*(Note: New Amazon commissions will make the average payout amount small than what is reflected here. -PV)*

Let's take a nervous seller, someone who prices a textbook for $10 FBA. They get a $4 payout.

Now let's take someone who's is slightly more aggressive, not extremely so, just slightly more aggressive with their pricing, they take that textbook and they price it at $19 and they get a $12 payout. That is three times the return for only what I would consider to be slightly more aggressive pricing practice. *Three times the return.*

Let's say someone buys textbook and they price it at $14.99 and they get an $8 payout. Then let's say you got somebody else who takes that same textbook and prices it at $30 and they get a $24 payout. *Three times the return.*

Again, we're not getting like too insane with our pricing. You know, they price at double the amount of the first person, a nervous seller, but it's not too crazy.

Another example of a nervous seller, someone who prices their textbook at $20, gets a $13 payout and then somebody priced that same book at $50 and gets a $40 payout. Again, *three times the return.*

So what did we just see? Slightly bolder pricing but triple the revenue just by tweaking their pricing strategy a little. That's how important this stuff is. I can't stress this enough.

So why is nobody talking about pricing? I feel like there's kind of a black out amongst Amazon sellers when it comes to pricing.

One, I think it's just not an exciting subject so people don't really like to talk about it even though it's so important. It's subjective and I never claimed that the formula I'm about to teach is the "right way," I think it's a better way than what most people do but it's not a hard and fast formula that you can apply in every situation and just go on autopilot. It's a very fluid thing, so it's hard to teach.

It's also very complicated. You've got to consider at least six different variables when you're pricing just to know what the optimal price should be. So it's not simple.

If you've been listening to me for any length of time, I get kind of conspiratorial sometimes. And I do have a conspiracy theory about this, like why there's a virtual blackout on the subject of pricing even though it's where you stand to make or lose the most amount of money. I think that a lot of these self-professed gurus who are out there just want your money and they want to sell you things but they want you to like them too. And they know that there's really no money in selling delayed gratification. So the pricing formula that I'm about to teach you requires some delayed gratification. You're not going to get the instant sales as soon as your stuff hits the warehouse, I mean you might actually in August but the generally the rest of the year, you're not going to get instant sales if you price the way I'm going to tell you to price. But you will make a lot more money.

And most people are just inherently lazy and they will absolutely turn on anyone that has the gall to suggest they shouldn't get instant returns for their work. You know those people who want to push the button on the computer and have money pour out of it, the get rich quick mentality, people I don't really care to do business with or even be friends with.

Those kinds of people are who most gurus cater to and they know you cannot cater to that lowest common denominator if you sell delayed gratification, which is what my pricing strategy requires.

So if there's more money in selling instant results and pandering to an audience even if ultimately that message is a detriment to the profits of the people they're supposed to serve.

So it is a fact you will get more sales if you price like a moron but you will make less money. I don't know about you, I'm here to make money, not sales.

So if we're all on that page and I hope we are, let's get into my pricing formula.

Oh, this is just so funny, just to drive home this point. Someone send me a video recently. It was an embarrassment. I don't pay attention to most of what these self-identified gurus teach, I don't even know who most of these guys are. But man, some of the stuff is embarrassing. Someone sent me a video where this guy had, I swear he had like 2,000 YouTube followers. So I think he might even be somebody that you guys follow, I would mention his name if I could remember it, I actually don't.

But he had a bunch of followers and someone sent me a link to this video and it had like 3,000 views. So people are definitely watching it. And it was this guy attempting with a straight face to teach what he considered to be his super ninja textbook pricing formula. And he said, and this is totally with a straight face, I can't believe people fall for the stuff. It's embarrassing. But this guy actually said, "Okay, here's what you do." He said, he said, "You look at the Keepa chart with the Keepa extension." He said, "You take the lowest merchant fulfilled used price, then you take the highest new merchant fulfilled and you price your FBA offer right in the middle. And that is the magic formula for getting the most amount of money for your textbooks."

And I'm just sitting there and my jaw is on the floor, like I can't believe people listen to this stuff. It's completely insane. There is so much bad information out there. I mean there's a black out on talking about it but the people who do talk about it don't know what they're talking about. And I don't want to sound like, "Hey, everybody, listen to Peter Valley and don't listen to anyone else." Listen to what works, okay? When I describe this formula I'm going to teach you, if it doesn't work, by all means, feel free to call me a liar. All I can say is I've practiced this for many years and it's working very well for me. And I believe I make more money off textbooks than the average seller.

## The Ultimate Textbook Pricing Formula

So with that editorial out of the way, any intelligent pricing formula is going to rely on five variables.

Just so it's clear, the eventual selling price can never be predicted. There's no way to ever know what something is going to sell for. Which is why that video that I watched was so insane. There's no perfect pricing formula but there are formulas that will make you a lot more money than others.

So the "right price" is a relationship between the five different variables:

- Sales rank history
- Merchant fulfilled price
- FBA price
- Amazon's price
- Type of book

In this case, were talking about textbooks so we don't even need to acknowledge that one now.

But with basically with textbooks, it's four variables you need to look at before you can set a price. You can size all these up in literally a split second most of the time. So it's not like you have to pull out a whiteboard to know what to price a textbook at. But if you're not factoring in each of these into your pricing formula, it's too simplistic.

So I'm going to make this very simple for you and you're leaving a ton of money on the table by the way if you don't consider all five of these things.

## The Most Important Fact About Pricing Textbooks

Textbooks follow a totally different pricing law than all other books. I can't stress this enough.

*As an FBA seller, you can price textbooks insanely higher than non-FBA offers and still get sales.*

So this is a totally different set of rules than what applies to normal books. Depending on the sales rank, there's almost no limit to how aggressively you can price a high demand textbook and still get sales, in the absence of competing FBA offers.

So most people don't really believe this until they try it but then when they try it, they're like "Wow." Once they suspend their disbelief and actually price a $15 merchant fulfilled book for $50 and get a sale, they're like "Wow, that's pretty cool."

So there's three reasons this works. Three reasons the FBA sellers can price textbooks like bandits and still get away with it.

Number one, urgency. A lot of times, professors will say, "Okay, here's your syllabus, here's the books you need to buy. You need to have these by Monday," and it's Thursday. And students cannot wait for a merchant fulfilled book. They have to have that book in their hands by Monday. So they can go to the university bookstore, which they may do, but today they're more likely just to go on Amazon and buy it via Prime.

Also consider students may get their syllabus well in advance, but most procrastinate. So they wait until the last minute, and then really need that textbook by a certain date, and its urgent.

Number 2, Amazon student program or Amazon Prime for college students, they get a discounted rate.

And Number 3, some mystical factors that none of us really understand but we all make a lot of money off of it. A think the biggest hidden factor here is that many if not most students are having their parents pay for everything, so they have no skin in the game as far as how much they spend on textbooks. It doesn't impact them at all, and they're happy to blow their parents money, so they spend $100 on a textbook they could have paid $20 for.

The one mantra you have to chant yourself is,

*"With textbooks, people pay way way more for FBA offers than in any other category."*

So here it is, my textbook pricing formula.

I need to give this big disclaimer. What I'm about to show you is *in the absence of any other FBA offer* which realistically is not going to happen very often. Most textbooks have multiple competing FBA offers. So if you have the luxury of having a book that has no competing FBA offers, this next slide is how I would price a textbook like that.

- If the rank was 1 to 30,000, I would price $50 to $100 above the lowest non-FBA offer.
- If the rank was 30k to 150,000, I would price $40 to $70 higher.
- If the rank was 150k to 300k, I'd price $35 to $50 above.
- If it was 300,000 to 600,000, I would price $30 to $40 above.
- If it was 600,000 to 900,000, I would do somewhere in range of $25 to $35 above.

And as the years have gone on, I have been more sort of liberal about this pricing formula. You notice these numbers have gone up over the years that I've been teaching the stuff. It's because they keep going higher and I keep getting sales.

So this stuff does work and you've just got to suspend your disbelief.

I need to point out, sales rank is a fluid thing. There is no magic line that's crossed between going from 30,000 to 30,001 in terms of sales rank but you have to have a formula. It's more about hedging your bets than that 30,000 or 150,000 number have any inherent meaning. It's just about if you had to create a formula this is generally where I am. It's not necessarily you need to scribble this down and adhere to this to the letter.

So like I said, textbooks with no competing FBA offers are very hard to find. So how do you price a textbook when you're up against a bunch of FBA sellers? This is how I go about it. When it's just before textbook season like the time, like right now when I'm recording this, it's a delicate balance of not pricing too low but not pricing yourself off the first page either. So you've got to strike that balance. There's no hard science to this which is why it's very difficult to teach. But I'm going to do my best and just keep in mind this is a fluid thing. This is not etched into a tablet somewhere.

When a book has an average rank of 1-30,000, I'll price in the off season 5th or 6th lowest. So I will go way down the page when a book is really well ranked.

If it's 30k to 300k roughly, I'll go to 4th or 5th lowest.

When it's 300k to 600k, I'll go 3rd or 4th.

When it's 600k to 900k, I'll go 2nd or 3rd.

I'll consider if any competing offers are Acceptable because a lot of buyers will skip Acceptable condition books.

I also check and adjust my prices daily during textbook season.

After the peak, once you clear the third week in August in this upcoming textbook season, if you're not in the top three lowest prices after the third week of August, that's when I start to drop my prices to make sure I'm in the top or in the bottom two or three.

That's unless you're dealing with books in the top sales rank strata. And in that case, you know that their prices are so volatile your book's going to sell no matter what. It almost doesn't matter what you do with it. You don't want to get too far down the page but you can not be so thorough with books that are really well-ranked.

Then I get progressively more conservative with my prices as I move towards the end of the textbooks rush.

Now, it doesn't mean I'm desperate to have every textbook sell during the textbook season. I don't want to paint that picture. In fact, I don't get too concerned at all. I don't even know my numbers as to what percentage sells during a textbook season. I don't even care that much. I know that after two textbooks seasons passed, I would say definitely the majority of my textbooks in my inventory should have sold. But I'm not so concerned about whether or not they sell after any one season.

## Repricing Strategy

Now a general repricing formula. This is where you're going through and repricing stuff after it hits the Amazon warehouse.

You've heard me say this before hopefully. If this is the first time, I feel strongly about this: Do not ever, ever trust your textbooks or most other books to repricing software ever, ever, ever. It doesn't work, I can go into detail in the Q&A if you want but it does not work. And it's not like this is my opinion, this is absolute fact that it simply they cannot see FBA offers if they're not in the bottom 20. So I can expand on that later if you want.

Third-party software has massive blind spots. Be extremely, extremely careful…in fact, just don't use it for textbooks at all, period. Ever, ever, ever.

General repricing guidelines: Reprice textbooks less often than normal books. Reprice textbooks less often than normal books in the offseason because again, prices are going to go up in the textbook season so you don't need to be that diligent. And it doesn't mean ignore them but just don't reprice them as often. And then when textbook season hits, so you know when you're approaching mid August, start to reprice your textbooks daily or multiple times daily to keep them price-optimized.

Again, you're just as often increasing the prices as lowering the prices. In fact, this is much more about raising prices for your textbooks as it is about lowering them during textbook season because you don't want to get caught with a book that sells for less that what it could have sold for. But during textbook season, you're checking prices often to raise them as often as lower them.

A couple last things on pricing before we get to textbook sourcing. At the time of listing, code your SKUs of all textbooks for easy repricing. So you can do that in any listing software you have or if you list through Amazon. You could just put a keyword in there like "textbook" for example and the SKU, the merchant SKU, so that it's easy to go back in at a glance and reprice using whatever tool you want. Go ahead and reprice the textbooks based on searching for the textbook SKUs.

A ton of textbooks are just not going to sell over any one textbook season. It's not a big deal. Don't freak out. It doesn't mean you did anything wrong. Again, unless, and I've said this before, but unless you've got a heroin needle in your arm right now, you don't need to get too concerned about getting having everything sell right away and treat it like its some kind of crisis. It's not a crisis. It shouldn't be a crisis and you shouldn't expect everything to sell right away.

Recap

- Price high
- Price really high
- The biggest factors in pricing are not anything other than sales rank and other FBA offers Don't trust repricers except maybe Amazon's repricer.
- Price daily during textbook season
- Reprice less often in the offseason
- If you reprice diligently, most textbooks are going to sell over a six-month period

# Textbook Pillar III

# Textbook Sourcing

# Textbook Pillar #3: Textbook Sourcing

Okay, so now we're into even more fun stuff. We're going to get into sourcing.

To talk about textbook sourcing is really to talk about all book sourcing in general. Because anywhere you go, anywhere you're going to get books, there's going to be the chance there's textbooks. So that is a massive subject.

I have a book about it called *Book Sourcing Secrets*. It would be redundant to get into a complete massive tutorial on the dozens and dozens of places where you can source books. What I decided to do here is reveal a place where source books in one location in about eight different ways, a place that has the highest concentration of textbooks anywhere in the world.

So this is the single best source of textbooks in the universe, and within this source, there seven different angles you can take to get tons of textbooks with one stop.

**All Amateurs Go For Textbooks First**

But first of all, it is basically a very amateur mindset to say the money in Amazon book selling is in textbooks. All amateurs go right for the textbooks. That is the lowest hanging fruit. That is the lowest common denominator of book target for people, and you see this time and time again. You know when you go to a library book sale and as soon as the doors swing open, all the sellers hit the door running and just dog pile on the textbooks? Mistake.

Pick any "low hanging fruit" source, let's say a thrift store, textbooks are always the first books to go. A lot of people go to these sources and they only go for the textbooks, they don't go for anything else. That makes valuable textbooks, somewhat difficult to find in the second hand market.

So it's an example of low order Amazon thinking to say textbooks are where the money is. I want to get you out of that mindset, okay. Don't focus too much on textbooks but ask yourself, "Where's the highest concentration of textbooks in the world that almost nobody is tapping into?"

What I want to do with this section is to give you a single source where you can nearly always find tons of textbooks, that the amateurs are almost certainly not touching.

I call this my "University-Centric Sourcing Model."

Universities, they're the number one. That's where the textbooks are. You heard of, was it

Willie Sutton or Willie Dutton, who is the guy that robbed the banks? In court they asked him, "Sir, why did you rob banks?" And he said very profoundly, "Banks are where the money is."

Well, universities are where the textbooks are. So there are eight sources of textbooks by my count on any university campus.

Even if you don't think you have a college near you, you do. So it's just a matter of finding and going there. Each one of these would apply to any college campus. So no matter where you are in the country, it would pay to pay attention to this.

Now these eight I'm going to talk about, each one of them individually isn't necessarily a gold mine but the fact that you can go to a college campus and have eight different options of places to source books on any campus is significant. So you can in one swoop hit seven different types of sources on one campus and you're definitely going to come away from any college campus with some opportunity. I'm going to go rapid fire into what these are.

They are:

1. University library ongoing sales
2. Regular library book sales
3. University library culled books
4. University library dumpsters
5. University bookstore bargain bins
6. University press offices
7. University surplus stores
8. Professor's offices

**University library ongoing sales and regular book sales**

These are actually relatively uncommon. I want to be clear about that. I've found them, definitely a significant number of times in my book selling career. But I will mention that these aren't totally common. But when they're good, they're really good. So you might go to ten libraries and only get one hit but man, when you find one that has an ongoing sale or some sort of like monthly book sale or something… When they're good, they're really good.

Remember that any large university is going to have multiple libraries. The university across the street from my house has a main library, a math library, a law library, a business library, a sciences library, and probably others I haven't discovered yet. When you visit a campus, you want to hit every library.

**So university libraries and capitalizing on books that are culled from their stacks.** The way you do this, you go to the front desk and you say, "Hey, what do you do with the books that you pull from your stacks that are pulled from circulation?" They're probably going to tell you they go to the university surplus department. That's the most common scenario. They probably will never tell you that they go in the trash, which happens a lot. But if they tell you that they're not throwing away lots of books constantly, they are totally lying.

So the point of all this is your goal is don't stop until you get an answer as to where their culled books go. They could have met their fate in several different ways but keep calling, keep going to the library until you get an answer.

**The next stop is the university library dumpster.** Even if you have reservations about dumpster diving, which a lot of people do, I think you'll be pleasantly surprised both at how consistent library dumpsters are in terms of books and how orderly they are as in you're not going to be dealing with apple cores and fish heads. They can be pretty clean dumpster diving experiences.

Ideally, you can work out a way to intercept books pre-dumpster but if not, the dumpster is where a lot of books meet their fate. And I've made many tens of thousands of dollars at this point off of university library dumpsters, so it's absolutely a lucrative source if you can get over any sort of the hang-ups that you might have.

**Next stop is on your university recon trip is the university bookstore bargain bin.** This is actually uncommon for the simple reason that most university bookstores already have an arrangement with some sort of third-party as to how they liquidate the books that they don't sell anymore. And this is driven largely by the fact that Barnes & Noble, most people don't even know this, but Barnes & Noble owns the majority of college bookstores in this country. They're actually secretly owned by Barnes & Noble. I always wondered what happened to the books they pull from their bookstores. I don't know the answer to that.

Most large universities have an arrangement with large companies who liquidate their throwaways. Especially the smaller college bookstores, they can have bargain bins where they just dump all the textbooks they consider to be obsolete. These can be great source of books that may not have any merchant fulfilled value but still have great FBA value.

**University press office.** Most larger colleges will have a university press that prints books. Now these are not necessarily textbook sources but these are sources of books that have a demand on college campuses and they're just a good source of books in general.

So what I would do is go find out where their office is. Actually often times it's not on campus. Go in there and find out if they do overstock sales. Find out what happens to their back catalogue. Find out how they liquidate slow-selling titles. It might be a simple matter of calling or even just knocking on the door and just saying, "Hey, do you guys ever have regular sales where you purge your back catalogue or what have you? How do you get rid of the old stuff you don't want anymore?" Again it's a case where you don't want to stop until you get an answer. And hopefully, you will get an answer.

**University surplus stores.** These are super cool and a lot of people don't even know they exist. This is an actual photo from the Oregon State University surplus store. This is a major source.

Universities liquidate surplus in one of several ways. One is a surplus store like you see here. Second one is a regular auction. Third one is an online auction or they contract to some third party that does God knows what with their stuff. But all universities have tons and tons of surplus. They all have tons and tons of books they need to liquidate and they all do it in one way or another. So it's just a question of finding how they liquidate their surplus. And these can actually be great sources of non-book inventory too. It's amazing what you'll find at these places.

**Next stop is my favorite of all: Professors offices.** Here's the formula: Pick a department, create a flyer with your phone number and email, preferably a website. I have a flyer that just says, "Hey, you've got too many books. Let me buy them from you. Here's my number, I pay competitive rates and I make it easy on you and I won't take much of your time and you can have cash in hand within 20 minutes." That's basically what my flyer says. Then you go to a university building at night, after hours. I go at night and I slide these under the door of every single office in a particular building. Most buildings are unlocked long after the professors go home. Then you sit back and wait for the phone calls or emails to come in. It's really that simple.

If a campus is big enough, they're going to have 30 different department buildings and there is virtually no end to the supply. This can be really lucrative. I'll offer a percentage of the expected profits or a flat rate if they just want me to take all of their books. If they just say, "I just want everything on the shelf gone," I'll make them a really low ball flat rate for that without cherry picking the collection.

You can make a lot of money doing this.

And that is how you get a limitless supply of textbooks from the biggest textbook source in the world.

# Audience Q&A

# Questions and Answers

**"Before sending it to Amazon, do you remove stickers with the very low price written on them?"**

Yeah, I do. That's a great question, Kyle. So Kyle is asking if you source books in the second hand market, do you remove stickers that indicate that you paid a small amount for them less as than the buyer's paying? I always do because I do think you run the risk of offending people who feel...and it's silly. But people feel like you're kind of getting one over on them if they see that $1 price sticker so I do think it's important to remove those. All other stickers I pretty much ignore except for the price stickers.

**"I know bottom line is sales, but is there a rank too high or too many competitors to sell a textbook in Amazon?"**

So Tammy, here's my answer to that. I personally don't like to mess with a textbook if I've seen it ranked worse than 1.7-ish million at anytime other than mid December. Now if I'm sourcing online, I like the number to be 1.2. It's very subjective. I don't want you to like tattoo this on your face or anything. This is very subjective. And the reason it's lower with online sourcing for me or more conservative is that you are investing more. By the nature of the fact the cheapest you can pay in Amazon is $4. I like to have a little more insurance that book's going to sell but a lot of books that are 1.7 million could spike during textbook season so I'm still not too put off by that. So that's a short answer to that question, Tammy.

**"What's going on with the corrector's proof copies?"**

Here's my rule of thumb with all textbooks. This could hopefully be a benefit to people because it answers a lot of these questions. If there's a product page for it on Amazon already, I will list it. If I'm uncertain as to whether or not I'm allowed to sell it or there's some kind of ambiguity there, if there's a product page for it, I'll list it. If there's not, I won't. That's the safest way to go about it.

Amazon can never fault you for listing something that they allow a product page to exist for. So if you use that as kind of just a baseline rule of thumb as to whether or not it's okay to list a book, you'll do just fine. Now, the pitfall there is that you could potentially miss out on a lot of books that you could have created a product page for but if you just want to err on the side of caution, if there's a preexisting product page, you are not liable for what Amazon allows to exist on their website.

**"How do you price books not listed on Amazon?"**

That is a good question. So Theresa, if you're asking about books that literally don't have any offers, I do $100 to $500 and I've sold to date 6 or 7 books at $500. So books at that price will sell and I'm actually doing an article about this on FBA Mastery very soon because I think there is formula you can apply. If you're the only seller, how do you know whether to list at 100 or 500? Or heck, a thousand. I've never done it but you know you could. Or even less than a hundred sometimes. So there is a formula there but I would, as a general rule of thumb, I would list it a hundred but if it's a book that I think can get more using my formula, which I'll go into this article.

**"How much do you offer to pay for professors books?"**

So the way I do that is I am basically... 20% of your expected profit. What I'll do is I have FBA Scan and I'll add like add to button, you know you can click the buy list or whatever it is. And then it calculates your net profit and then I'll basically offer them 20% of that.

Occasionally, people would just say I just want all these books gone and you can just offer them a really lowball rate. And basically if they say they want all these books gone or they're trying to offer, they want you to get rid of all their books that's basically their way of saying you're doing more for me than I'm doing for you. So that's your invitation to make a very low-ball offer.

**"What is your basic flyer info that you slide in to professors' doors at universities? My internet cut-out when you're explaining that."**

So basically, it just says, the headline says, "You have too many books." The subtitle says, "I will buy them." It's got my name, number and it says something about an email address and I'll say something about "So you have multiple ways to contact me," and then it says something about how I will give you cash in hand in under 20 minutes. Basically, emphasize that I will make this very convenient for them and just real simple, professional, make it look good and multiple ways to contact you, emphasize convenience. And then that's it. Pretty straight forward.

**"I don't understand when you said when you say 'code your SKUs' for easier repricing."**

So basically what you do is you have the option of however you list through whether it's third party software or through Amazon, you have the option of basically making up your own SKU. So I just put the word "text" in all my textbooks SKUs. So then when I go on to Amazon to manually reprice, I will put the word text in as a search and it just brings up my textbooks. So then at a glance, with just one keyword search I can bring up only my text books, which again, repricing according to a totally different set of rules. And then from that point, I just go ahead and then just go down the line and reprice. So it's just about putting the keyword or it can be anything that you can search within Amazon within you inventory listing to bring just those books up.

### "Peter, anyone else tried emailing the professors offering to buy their books?"

What I have heard people doing that I have not done is hiring people to go door-to-door or just going door-to-door like during office hours. I'm not quite that bold so but I bet that would convert much better. So emailing, you'd probably get, you know I'm guessing a lower response rate even than a flyer but man you can do it all from your computer. So just give and take.

### "Regarding the Goodwill price stickers, is it necessary to really remove the remained sticky residue?"

Man, that is in the bottom one million things I think we should be worried about and focus our time on. I really don't see any value in that at all.

Mike's asking again about the...he is responding to the question about removing sticky residue. Here's my thing. I think that you can easily get caught up as an Amazon seller. It's not that removing sticky residue hurts you, it's that you've got a finite amount of time and you should focus on the one or two things that generates the most amount of profits and not ever do anything that could potentially risk your standing with Amazon but understand that when good enough is good enough.

So removing sticker residue is definitely one of those things where I believe you're getting caught up in distractions. I'll put it this way. No mega seller, these people that the 50,000 feedback rating, none of these people have a team of people with W-40 scrubbing books. And yeah, their feedback might be 94-95% and ours might be 98%, but honestly, it's worth it to avoid the mountain of labor you subject yourself to if you're trying to clean every book. So my position with business is just focus on the most highly leveraged stuff, the sourcing, and the pricing and ignore all those details.

### "Do you add creases or no crease in your condition notes?"

No, I don't. I don't really get too particular. I think highlighting is the one thing I'd like to mention with textbooks is whether or not it has highlight. Obviously, mention any blemishes. But as far as the absence of blemishes, I don't really know acknowledge anything like that. It takes a lot of time honestly to cater each listing description.

**"I find textbooks that are clean on the covers but dirty on the outside of the pages and often mark with names in black markers. Books are clean on the inside where it matters. Is it okay to sell as acceptable? Reading Amazon's policy on selling clean items is a little confusing."**

Okay. So Don, if you're just dealing with a book that's clean on the inside and has some markings on the outside, there's no reason that to sell that, to grade that lower than Good. I would list a book like that as Good especially it was clean on the inside. In fact, Good condition can even allow of a certain amount of highlighting on the inside. You know if it's over 15-20 pages, you might start to think about listing it as acceptable.

But yeah man, there's no reason to get too caught up on that stuff. That sounds like a Good condition book to me, if not possibly very good, probably good. If you have any doubts, err on the side of grading conservatively. But yeah, man. That's nothing wrong with that at all. I don't think anyone's going to be too concerned about that. I mean if you had like a ton of writing and it was just a big mess, it's something to consider.

**"Does anyone been mad that you got in their dumpster?"**

Here's the thing. If you can have any sort of any confrontation, first of all it's like completely a ridiculous human being. It's never gonna be like you're in the wrong and you've got something to feel bad about. It's like trash. It's literally the end of the line before the landfill. Anyone that has an issue with you being in or near their dumpster doesn't deserve your respect. I generally just end up making fun of people rather than cowering. So don't worry about that.

Like when I was out dumpster diving at the end of the college semester a couple months ago, this college kids they're like you know well kind of like laugh at you. I had a kid in his dorm that yell, "Get out of the dumpster." You know, I'm like, "Make me," or whatever.

Anyway, the point is this is pretty much a non-issue. I wouldn't worry about it. It's been years. But like maybe a million years ago, I've had some cops called on me on a bunch of occasions but never for books. I mean, it's just pretty much not going to happen.

**"Are you offering the professor 20% of the merchant fulfilled or the FBA?"**

I offer professors 20% of what I expect to profit is the answer to that question.

**"A bestseller rank alone doesn't necessarily reflect good sales velocity. I've come across very good rank but sales volume is low. How do you approach this?"**

It's all in the average sales rank, Lori. So that's it. I mean, and you can get that in Keepa, you can get that in Camel, you can get that in Zen Arbitrage, you can get that in FBA Scan. It's all there. So that's it. So you know, again, you just want to see on average what is something and then you know, it's also good to look at what's the worst that it's been to get an idea about how long a book goes between selling. But that's pretty much it. It's really shouldn't be anymore complicated than that.

**"How do you package the books in your shipments to Amazon? Poly bags, bubble-wrap?"**

Okay. Zack get out the whiteboard. I'm going to give you the master formula for shipping books, you're ready? Get out your pen, get your whiteboard, get out two whiteboards.

So draw a picture of a box and then draw picture of a book and then draw an arrow from the book to box and then picture me putting tape over the box. And that is literally as complicated as I make it.

So that's a long way of saying you just put the book in the box and tape it shut. I've never, ever poly bagged a book. I've never bubblewrapped a book.

That is the biggest, one of the biggest waste of time. I don't know where these rumors get started. And I don't mean to sound like whatever. I don't mean to belittle your question but there's a lot of just wacky people especially on Facebook who will insist you have to literally put your book on a gilded pillow and have it carried to Amazon by angels. It's not necessary.

Again, do what you're comfortable with but the only time I get a little bit concerned is when I'm shipping new books to Amazon. And even in that instance, I'm really not that concerned. I'll never wrap anything and all I means I'll do is put the books in smaller boxes so there's less wiggle room literally and so there's less jarring and corners getting bumped and stuff. But that's it, Zack. That's really it. I would definitely go head-to-head in any debate with anybody who wanted to make it more complicated than just putting the book in a box and then shipping it.

**"Do you think a seller's feedback still relevant when it comes to selling via FBA?"**

I think you're asking, "Does it affect sales?" Nobody knows. My personal opinion is I don't think it affect sales that much but it...presumably somebody might be willing to pay $0.50

more to get a book from somebody who's got 98% versus someone who has 90%. Maybe. I don't know but I really wouldn't sweat that stuff that much. I mean look at any mega seller's feedback. Like there's no mega seller on Amazon that has feedback other than...I mean, very few are better than 95%. Most of them have like 90-94%. And they're still killing it.

**"How do you adjust your price for conditions worse than very good?"**

The answer is I don't at all. I will very rarely price lower than the lowest FBA offer. I will usually not at all factor in condition when it comes to pricing between good and like new. When it's acceptable, I only factor that in if I'm...and those will sell slower, don't get me wrong. But I don't like to get in a game of pricing from the heels, so to speak. So pricing from the heels just means pricing from a defensive place as in like, "Oh, I'm worried this isn't going to sell." Like I like to price with confidence. So I will price, even I will generally not even acknowledge that something is acceptable. I still acknowledge it's not going to sell as fast but it doesn't mean I'm going to price lower. So I don't really factor in condition that much. I just don't think you have to. It's all about just pricing something with confidence and knowing it will sell eventually.

**"Put your book,"** Judith says, **"On a gilded pillow and have it shipped to Amazon by angels. Please do not leave that out of the transcript."**

I'm glad you appreciate my ad lib. I think it's worth the occasional gem for all my bad jokes that are peppered in between.

"Laughing out loud at the gilded pillow," Josh says.

**"Do you price these types of books much differently than normal college textbooks if the prices and sales rank history are the same? College study guides, solution manuals, and or lab manuals. How about textbooks for middle school or high schools students for teachers versus textbooks for the middle?"**

Okay. So here's my answer to all that. So for the first three, the college study guides, solution manuals and lab manuals, those are textbooks 100%. Treat them exactly like textbooks. For middle school and high school students, I don't really know. I don't do enough business in those. I do a fair amount of business but not enough to be able to say conclusively how much...if they follow the same pricing rules as regular textbooks. I price them as though they do and they sell slower than textbooks but I also deal in lower volume.

Anyway, this is a very unsatisfying answer, Kyle. I don't know the answer to that. I basically err on the side of caution. So I do price high school textbooks and middle school textbooks generally the same way I do textbooks but I don't do enough volume in that type of book to really be able to say conclusively.

But you know, here's the thing and someone brought this up earlier. You can always lower your price later. You can't go back and get money from somebody who paid less than what you think they should have paid. So why not start high and by all means, monitor your inventory. If you're sitting on something for eight, nine, ten months or a year, you definitely start to adjust your pricing formula.

Okay. So you guys, that is it. That's the end of the questions as far as I've seen.

Thank you guys so much for being here.

So yeah, again, I really hope you guys can do well with the material I shared. And here's my approach to webinars: If you just get one gem out of all the stuff I talked about, that can pay dividends for a lifetime. So hopefully, you can at least get one thing, hopefully a lot of things out of this webinar. So thank you guys so much. I really appreciate your time. And I will catch you on the next one.

# Webinar Slides

# Textbook Annihilation

Everything there is to know about profiting off **textbooks** & **textbook season**

## The three pillars of textbook season profits

**1. Textbook Intelligence**

Understanding Textbooks

➡

**2. Textbook Pricing**

Optimizing Your Prices for Maximum Profits

➡

**3. Textbook Sourcing**

Where to Find Textbooks.

# Who am I?

My name is Peter Valley. Amazon seller since 2007.

I do the website www.FBA mastery.com (since 2013).

Authored many books & courses, including:

- *Amazon Autopilot* (over 5,000 copies sold)
- *Online Book Arbitrage* (over 5,000 copies sold)
- *Amazon Altitude* (video course)

# Nevermind what I've done, what motivates me?

I am 100%, firmly, unapologetically against working for anyone else.

That's why I do what I do.

The highest and most noble of personal goals is freedom.

That's what this selling with FBA - and this webinar - is about.

## When we reach the end...

You will learn:

- A deep knowledge of textbooks.
- How to price textbooks for maximum profits.
- The best sources of textbooks.
- Tons of Q&A.

## I started out as the worst, most inefficient Amazon seller ever

Whatever you're doing, I've done it worse.

I drove 45 minutes to garage sales because they said "box of books."

I drove an hour to buy 3 boxes of 1990s computer books.

I skateboarded 30 minutes to a college dumpster daily that only had books 1 out of 5 times I went.

I spent the first year as a seller keying in books manually on my flip phone.

# Textbook Profits Pillar #1:
## Textbook intelligence

## "Textbook intelligence" is defined as...

"The complete body of knowledge to identify textbooks, understand the textbook buyer, and the market forces that drive sales."

## What we're going to cover in this section:

- The myth of "textbook season"
- What textbook buyers care about
- What textbook buyers don't care about
- Do older editions sell?
- Condition and textbooks
- "Textbooks in disguise"- Spotting textbooks that aren't really textbooks
- Where Amazon sellers lose the most money with textbooks
- How to describe your textbooks
- Peak days of textbook season
- And more...

## How big is the textbook market?

**Total number of 2 and 4 year schools (2015):**
7,253

**Total number of students (2017)**
20.4 million.

# Lesson #1: Textbook season is a myth

(And it's partially my fault.)

Here's how most Amazon sellers look at textbook season:

*"The two times a year when people buy textbooks."*

How we should look at textbook season:

*"The two times a year when textbook sales go up."*

# Textbook season is a myth, cont'd

**Textbook sell all year round.**

If you're older, the world that existed when you were in school no longer exists.

Between online courses and general increased variety in higher education, textbooks are selling all year round.

The peaks of textbooks are no longer as high, and the lows of the "off season" aren't low at all.

If you think textbooks are a seasonal business - you're living in a world that no longer exists.

## That said, sales *will* spike in one week

**Textbook season lasts three weeks.**

**Fall semester:**
    This semester: Third week of August.
    Expect the biggest day to be August 20th.
    Expect the biggest week to be August 20th to 25th.

## Everyone wants to know...

- How many textbooks will I sell during textbook season?
- What percentage of my textbooks will I sell?
- How many textbooks do I need in my inventory to make $____?

*Asking these is to ask the wrong questions.*

Depends on: Pricing. Demand for your books. How regularly you reprice. Etc.

Focus on sourcing quality inventory & pricing effectively / regularly, rest takes care of itself.

# Do old textbooks sell?

The single most destructive question Amazon sellers get hung up on.

The age or edition of a textbook isn't just a lesser datapoint, it is literally 100% completely totally irrelevant.

**The age and edition of a textbook is meaningless.** 100% meaningless.

# The only thing that matters with measuring textbook sales...

1. Sales rank.

2. Sales rank history (Keepa & CCC).

*Nothing else.*

If you're holding a copy of the 12th edition of "Intro to Biology" publishing in 1998, and it is currently on its 326th edition - if the sales rank indicates it selling, its selling.

Never get hung up on what "makes sense" - shut off your brain & defer entirely to the data.

# Textbooks become obsolete over years, not semesters

Common myth:

*"Some of my textbooks aren't going assigned to students next semester, and I'm going to be stuck with worthless inventory."*

That's not how it works.

There is no such thing as a textbook that is on college syllabuses one semester, and vanishes the next semester.

There are 7,253 colleges in the United States - too many for there to be any course material uniformity.

# Factors that <u>don't matter</u> in determining textbook value

- Rental price.
- Kindle price.
- Prices on other sites (eBay, etc).

Assume that your buyer is only looking at the page your book is on.

# Should you wait until August to ship textbooks in?

Seasonal business tend to not be sustainable.

My approach:

Ship them in when you get them, and price them "unreasonably" high, depending on rank.

# Ignore all sales rank history data from mid-December.

Looking at the "worst rank" data in Keepa and CamelCamelCamel can be deceptive.

Textbooks are peculiar in that the "worst" rank is not very telling.

When looking at Keepa chart, dig into the graph and ignore the extremes to give accurate look at demand.

# What matters to textbook buyers, and what doesn't

**What doesn't matter as much as with other books:**

- Inserts.
- Condition.

**What does matter:**

- Absence of highlighting.

# Actual statistic:
Annual revenue Amazon sellers lose because they're afraid to list textbooks that don't have all inserts

# $1,000,000,000,000,000,000,000,000,000,000,000,000.

Don't contribute to this figure.

Inserts don't matter that much.

# What matters to textbook buyers, and what doesn't

I never hesitate to sell textbooks without CDs / access codes, nor do I mention their absence.

I will mention the *presence* of inserts.

My experience: Almost no one cares about access codes or inserts.

Bonus insurance: Amazon now includes disclaimer warning buyers that used books may not come with inserts.

# What doesn't matter (as much): Condition

With condition, textbook buyers are not nearly as particular as the general Amazon book buyer.

You will not see frivolous feedback like "*ordered a VG copy and received a G copy.*"

Generally, the textbook buyer is looking for an intact book that is free of highlighting (and they often won't even care about that).

You can relax your grading standards... Slightly.

# What does matter to textbook buyers

The biggest question textbooks buyers ask: *Does it have highlighting or not?*

If they feel strongly about highlighting, they probably aren't going to buy a book unless it clearly states "no highlighting."

I'm not saying most textbook buyers care that much, but the ones that do will pay more to avoid it.

Include "No writing or highlighting" front & center of any condition description.

# Highlighting is not a textbook death-sentence.

On the flipside: A lot of buyers prefer highlighting. It means someone has done the work for them.

I.e. Don't avoid a textbook because it has highlighting.

# Spotting "textbooks in disguise."

Most "textbooks" don't look like textbooks.

Most books purchased by students don't look like textbooks.

Learn how to spot books that are subject to the same market forces, but are "in disguise."

These are books that:

1. You can price insanely high.
2. Go way up in demand at the beginning of each semester.

# Spotting "textbooks in disguise, " cont'd

How to spot these:

- Niche non-fiction with no "real world" application (something no one would care about if they weren't forced to care).
- Books with those big square stickers on the back, or other markings.
- "Normal" books that have supplemental material like annotations, added analysis, etc.
- Non-fiction that generally appears scholarly and academic

*This is extremely important because the majority of "textbooks" fit into this category.*

# You are now have a genius level "textbook IQ"

- Textbook season is "glass half full" (not half-empty).
- Peak days for textbook sales.
- The truth about older textbooks.
- What textbook buyers care about, and what they don't.
- What matters most when describing your textbooks.
- Spotting textbooks in disguise.

# Textbook Profits Pillar #2: Pricing

# Why is textbook pricing important?

**Pricing is second only to your inventory** in what separates the people who make a lot of money, from the people who do "okay."

It's where most of your money is made in textbooks... and lost.

Two people with 500 textbooks: One will make 3x more than the other.

How? **Pricing.**

# Making the case: Comparing two pricing formulas

Nervous seller: $1 textbook priced $9.99 FBA: $2 payout.

Aggressive seller: $1 book priced $16.99: $7 payout.

   **3x the return.**

Nervous seller: $5 textbook priced $14.99 = $6 payout.

Aggressive seller: $5 textbook priced $29.99 = $18 payout.

   **3x the return.**

Nervous seller: $10 textbook priced $20 = $10 payout.

Aggressive seller: $10 textbook priced $50 = $40 payout.

   **4x the return.**

## Case closed.

Slightly bolder pricing.

*Triple the revenue.*

**Price + Shipping**
$49.95 ✓Prime
+ $0.00 estimated tax

**Condition** (Learn More)
Used - Good
some bent pages. Available for Prime Shipping

**Delivery**
FULFILLMENT BY AMAZON
- In Stock.
- Free Two-Day Shipping: Get it Wednesday, October 21 ( order within 23hr 5min )
- Domestic shipping rates and return policy

## Why is no one talking about pricing?

There is a virtual blackout on this subject among sellers.

1. It's not an exciting subject.
2. It's subjective. There is no "right way," so it's hard to teach.
3. It's complicated: At least 6 variables to consider.

## Theory: Why no one is talking about pricing

**Conspiracy theory:**

"Gurus" want your money.

There is no money in selling delayed gratification.

The "gurus" are teaching (i.e. selling) instant results, pander to their audience.

You will get more "sales" if you price like an amateur.

But you will make less money.

## How to spot a fraudulent pricing formula:
### One that is overly simplistic

Someone sent me a textbook pricing video from a "guru"... (Spoiler alert: it was bad).

Any intelligence pricing formula relies on 6 variables.

And the eventual selling price can *never* be predicted.

There is no "perfect pricing formula," but there are formulas that will make you a lot more money than others.

## The five factors of "the right price"

The right price is the relationship between 5 variables:

1. Sales rank history
2. Lowest merchant fulfilled price
3. Lowest FBA price
4. Amazon's price
5. Sometimes: The type of book

If you don't consider each of these when setting a price, you're leaving a ton of money on the table.

## All pricing rules go out the window with textbooks

Textbooks follow totally different pricing laws than other books

As a Fulfillment by Amazon seller, you can price textbooks *insanely* higher than non-FBA offers and still get sales.

There is almost no limit to how aggressively you can price a high-demand textbook.

Most people don't believe this until they try it.

# Three reasons for textbook pricing insanity

Three reasons FBA sellers can price textbooks like bandits and get away with it:

1) Urgency (people need their second-day shipping).
2) Amazon Student program (Amazon Prime for college students at a discounted rate).
3) Some mystical factors that none of us understand.

*"With textbooks, people will pay way, way more for FBA offers than in any other category."*

# My textbook pricing formula

When a book holds an average rank of...

1 to 30,000: Price $50 to $100 above the lowest non-FBA offer.

30,000 to 150,000: Price $40 to $70 above the lowest non-FBA offer.

150,000 to 300,000: Price $35 to $50 above lowest non-FBA offer.

300,000 to 600,000: Price $30 to $40 above lowest non-FBA offer.

600,000 to 900,000: Price $25 to $35 above.

# However, textbooks with no competing FBA offers are hard to find

How do you price a textbook when you're up against many FBA sellers?

When it's just before textbook season (like the time we're recording this), it's a delicate balance of not pricing too low, but not pricing yourself off the page.

There's no hard science to this, but here's how I do it...

# My pricing formula

When a book holds an average rank of...

   1 to 30,000: Price 5th or 6th lowest.

   30,000 to 300,000: Price 4th or 5th lowest.

   300,000 to 600,000: Price 3rd or 4th lowest

   600,000 to 900,000: Price 2nd or 3rd lowest.

Consider if any competing offers are Acceptable, and check prices *daily*.

# After the peak (3rd week in August)

If you're not in the top 3 lowest prices, drop prices to get there.

Unless you're dealing with books in the top strata (1 to 50,000).

Then get progressively more conservative with your prices as you move towards end of textbook rush.

# General repricing formula

Above all else: Do NOT ever ever ever trust your textbooks (or most other books) to repricing software. EVER.

Same applies to Amazon's repricer.

General guidelines:

- Price textbooks less often than normal books in the "off season."
- Price textbooks daily (or multiple times daily) during textbook season.

During textbook season, you are checking prices often to raise them more than lower them.

# Random pricing notes

1. At the time of listing, code SKUs of all textbooks for easy repricing.

2. I don't get the least bit concerned if a textbook doesn't sell during a textbook season.

3. Most will sell after two seasons. …but only if you're diligent about your repricing.

4. The way to conquer new fees is through superior pricing.

5. A <u>ton</u> of your textbooks won't sell during textbook season. This is not a big deal.

# Recap

- Price high.
- Price really high.
- Biggest factors in pricing are not anything other than: sales rank & other FBA offers.
- Don't trust repricers.
- Price daily during textbook season.
- Price less often during off-season.
- If you reprice diligently, most textbooks will sell over two textbook seasons.

# Textbook pillar #3: Sourcing

# Sourcing: All amateurs go for the textbooks

You'll see it time and again:

- Library book sale: Sellers hit the door running, and dogpile on the textbooks.
- "Low hanging fruit" sources: Textbooks are the first to go.

An example of low-order Amazon thinking: "Textbooks are where the money is."

Where is the highest concentration of textbooks that no one else is tapping into?

# "University-Centric Sourcing Model"

Eight sources of textbooks (and other books) on any university campus:

1. University library ongoing sales or regular book sales (rare but worth inquiring)
2. University library - culled books from stacks (inquire with front desk).
3. University library dumpster.
4. University bookstore "bargain bins"
5. University Press office.
6. University surplus store / department.
7. Professor's offices.
8. The biggest source of all...

# University library ongoing sales or regular book sales

These are relatively uncommon.

But if you go to 10 libraries and only get one hit, you've offset all the work you put in tenfold (when these are good, they're really good).

# University library - culled books from stacks

Ask the front desk: What do you do with discards, and books pulled from circulation?

They'll probably tell you they go to the university surplus department.

They'll probably never tell you they go in the trash (which they might).

If they tell you they don't throw away books, they're lying.

All libraries throw away books regularly - *get an answer as to where they go.*

## University library dumpster.

Even if you have reservations about dumpster diving, you might be pleasantly surprised at how both consistent and orderly college library dumpsters are.

Ideally you can work out a way to intercept them pre-dumpster.

## University bookstore "bargain bins"

Also uncommon, but worth investigating.

Most large universities have arrangement with large companies who liquidate their throwaways, or are owned by Barnes and Noble.

These bargain bins can be great sources of books that have no MF value, but still have FBA value.

## University Press office.

Not a "textbook source" per se, but if you're on a university campus already, worth inquiring.

Find out if they do overstock / back catalog sales, or how they liquidate slow selling or out of print titles.

## University surplus store / department.

Major source.

Universities liquidate surplus in one of several ways (or several of several ways):

1. Surplus store.
2. Regular auctions.
3. Online auctions.
4. Contract a third-party.

Find out which applies, and target it.

# Professor's Offices

Here's the formula:

1. Pick a department (i.e. Physics).
2. Create a flyer (w/phone number, email, and website)
3. Go at night and slide one under the door of every office (most buildings are unlocked long after professors go home).
4. Wait for inquiries.
5. Offer percentage of expected profit (20% is standard) or flat rate for large collection (lowball figure)

# And that (almost) concludes (almost) everything I know about textbooks.

CPSIA information can be obtained
at www.ICGtesting.com
Printed in the USA
BVHW011726011120
592172BV00006B/107